On The Edge

Extinct & Endangered Species:

Causes Behind It & Actions to Preserve

Anvesh Kolli

Table of Contents

1.Introduction

It's early morning in Kenya and under a wide African sky, the last two northern white rhinos left on Earth go for a stroll. From time to time, they pause; tasselled ears twitching, as they lower their broad, flat muzzles to nibble the parched grass. Najin and her daughter, Fatu, both live in Ol Pejeta Conservancy in Kenya and are the only two remaining northern white rhinos in the world. Sudan, the last remaining male, died on March 19th 2018, effectively rendering the entire subspecies extinct. The northern white rhino was once abundant across Central Africa, but staggering rates of illegal hunting for its horn have already led to its almost certain extinction in the wild. This makes the northern white rhino as good as gone, or, as scientists would call it, 'functionally extinct.' Najin and Fatu are 'dead rhinos walking.' The Bio Rescue project involves cutting-edge veterinary science, cell biology and the creation of test tube rhinos. If all goes according to plan, the pitter-patter of not-so-tiny rhino feet could be just a few years away. But the hope to happen so is not too high to be sure, we can only put efforts and trust the technology to come up with good results. It would be better to not create such critical situations in the first place where we are helpless due to our own doings.

There is a saying that goes like this "We usually don't value thing which are in our possession, we only come to know its true worth once we lose it". It can be a valuable object, relationship or even a living thing, so we need to be careful because sometimes it's too late even if we realize because, by then something irreversible may happen. Such a thing is the extinction of various plants and animal species due to us, humans. When a large number of species disappear during a relatively short period of time, this is referred to as a mass extinction. Extinction of any species is not a new thing, as many species have become extinct even before humans came into existence.

The largest extinction in Earth's history marked the end of the Permian period, some 250 million years ago. Permian-Triassic Mass Extinction or the Great Dying, where 90% of life in the oceans and 70% of life on land vanished. Long before dinosaurs, our planet was populated with plants and animals that were mostly obliterated after a series of massive volcanic eruptions in Siberia. Although life on Earth was nearly wiped out, the Great Dying made room for new organisms. Approximately 96% of marine species perished during the Great Dying, which was followed by millions of years during which life had to grow again and diversify, including the first dinosaurs.

After the great extinction earth again recovered and life again started to bloom so that was the time when dinosaurs used to roam on earth and they were at the top of the food chain at that time. Around 65 million years ago, another significant event occurred which resulted in the extinction of dinosaurs during the Cretaceous Period. There are several explanations proposed by scientists regarding what caused their extinction. However, among them all one theory has gained significant traction, that a large asteroid hitting Earth was primarily responsible for their demise. Scientists estimate that this asteroid may have been about 6 miles across and impacted what is now known as Mexico's Yucatan Peninsula leaving behind a massive crater. As per analysis performed by experts, it must have triggered many natural disasters like tsunamis and wildfire spread along with blocking out sunlight due to dust and debris causing global cooling leading up to their extinction.

Perhaps many could not imagine that their generation would witness the final disappearance of certain animal and plant species from the Earth, as part of what looks to be another mass extinction event to befall our planet. There are many reasons why, some of the animal species are gone extinct and while others are being pushed to extinction. But perhaps the main contributing factors include genetic variation, habitat loss, and other threats, especially humans.

Humans are a cause for extinction of animals since ancient times but in last few centuries we have been caused more species to become extinct. According to science, our planet is currently undergoing change at a rate that hasn't been observed in tens of millions of years. Oceans are becoming more acidic and oxygen-depleted, and species are disappearing as a result of overconsumption, unsustainable practices which result in production of enormous volumes of greenhouse gases from burning fossil fuels.

In the past few centuries, humans have already pushed countless creatures to extinction primarily as a result of hunting and the invasion of their natural habitats. As a result, certain animals are only now visible in written records, fossils, vintage photographs, museums, and history books.

Extinction is the death of all members of a species of plants, animals, or other organisms. According to recent studies, there are eight million species on Earth, at least 15,000 of which are in danger of going extinct. The precise extinction rate is difficult to determine because so many endangered species are still unidentified. Nearly all endangered species are in peril as a result of human activity alone. Early in the twenty-first century, it was argued that humans posed the biggest threat to biodiversity and were the main causes of its decline.

Many North American mammals went extinct during the end of the last ice age, 10,000 years ago, including mammoths, mastodons, and glyptodonts. In addition to climatic change, overhunting by humans was another contributing cause, according to palaeontologists' evidence. Early humans collaborated to catch and kill huge animals in pits. At around the same time, people started farming, moved in, and drastically altered other animals' habitats.

More than 16,000 of the 41,000 plant and animal species studied as of 2022 have been classified as endangered. According to experts, humans are the primary cause of the historically high rates of animal extinction. Increased food consumption, growth in construction and deforestation, an increase in pollution, overfishing and overhunting, and other issues are all results of an expanding human population. According to current estimates, species are vanishing up to 1,000 times faster than they did before the advent of humans.

Native species and habitat can be directly destroyed by development. Hundreds of thousands of acres have been removed by developers in South America's Amazon rain forest. In order to clear a piece of land, all of its trees and vegetation must be taken out. For logging, urban development, and livestock ranches, the Amazon rain forest is cleared. Development can also endanger species indirectly.

Some species, like the fig trees of the rain forest, might serve as a habitat for other creatures. As trees are destroyed, species that depend on that tree habitat may also become endangered. The same is true for numerous tropical bird species and mammals like monkeys. This habitat is being lost as trees are cut down. There is less space for species to thrive and reproduce.

In the last one to two decades, at least 32 species of Hawaiian birds that had persisted long enough to be recorded went extinct, and two more have uncertain status as separate species or subspecies. According to a 2016 study, it took an average of 12 years for a species to acquire protection. Several of the species mentioned in today's announcement became extinct while the listing process was delayed. At least 47 species have perished altogether while awaiting protection.

Today, only 17 species remain, most of which are restricted to small areas of habitat too cold for mosquitoes and avian disease. While habitat loss, invasive species, and non-native predators have negatively affected forest bird species for hundreds of years, and continue to do so, introduced diseases, particularly avian malaria, are the greatest threat to forest birds today. The new strategy of mosquito birth control program that aims to trim the number of disease-carrying insects that have invaded the birds forest habitats. It would also expand captive breeding efforts at enclosures safely removed from the malaria. Those approaches might not move quickly enough, however, to keep some of the most imperilled forest bird species from vanishing in the wild as others already have.

Almost all blooming plants in the tropical rainforest are pollinated by animals, and 75 percent of the world's food crops are partially or entirely pollinated by insects and other animals. A reduction in seed and fruit output from a lack of pollinators could ultimately lead to the extinction of many significant plants.

In order to keep species from going extinct, the discipline of conservation biology focuses on regulating ecosystems. Because we are limited in what we can conserve, conservation efforts concentrate on certain species or habitats. Questions concerning reviving extinct species have been raised by recent advancements in genetic engineering. Since Dolly the sheep was cloned in 1996, researchers are aware that it is feasible to develop an organism from a single cell's DNA. Extinct animal specimens with DNA are kept in museum collections all over the world.

The idea of using DNA to revive extinct species and repopulating them is controversial as we don't know the effects of few extinct species on the planet as they may not adjust to the new changes in climates and habitats. We saw a glimpse of this scenario in the famous film "Jurassic Park", where the outcome of bringing back few extinct dinosaurs brought disaster upon the people in the film as they didn't get accustomed to the setup created by current humans.

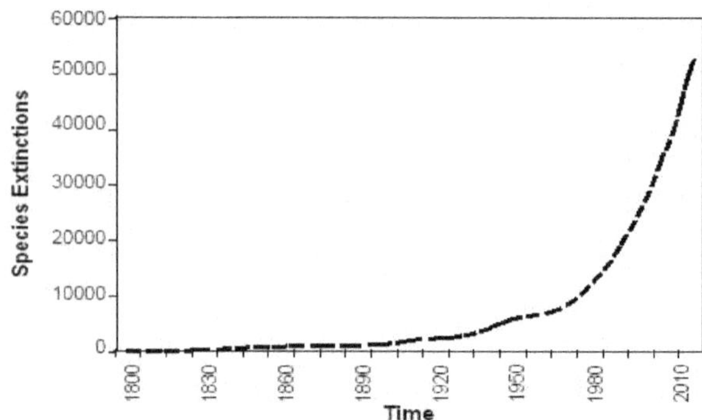

Fig: Graph indicating the no. of species that went extinct in last few centuries

2. Till 19th century

Ninety-nine percent of all species that have ever existed have vanished during the previously occurred mass extinctions, which historically were mostly brought on by purely natural events like asteroid impacts and volcanic eruptions. Due to human activity, the pace of extinction is now happening 1,000–10,000 times quicker. The primary contemporary causes of extinction include habitat loss and degradation, particularly deforestation, excessive hunting and fishing, the introduction of exotic species, climate change, and climatic pollution. Other dangers to animals include the widespread plastic pollution of the ocean that recent research discovered.

A single animal species' extinction can have profound impacts on its ecosystem and the surrounding environment. Every species is a vital component in a complex structure of interactions, and the extinction of one species can have a chain reaction that upsets the equilibrium of the entire ecosystem. First off, the extinction of a predator species can have an influence throughout the food chain. When only a few individuals remain and are incapable of procreating due to ill health, advanced age, sparse distribution over a wide range, a lack of members of both sexes, or other factors, a species may be considered functionally extinct.

Extinction may be natural, but it did not come easily to the naturalists. Species become extinct when they are no longer able to survive in changing conditions or against superior competition. Most species go extinct within 10 million years after their origin, however some, known as living fossils, can endure for hundreds of millions of years with little to no alteration. Out of 1,000 species that have existed, just one or two species are still in existence in such scenario. When the final member of an extinct species passes away, the species is declared extinct. When there are no living creatures left that can reproduce and pass on a new generation, extinction becomes inevitable.

The term "dark extinction" (DE), which refers to the extinction of species before they are discovered and given names, is frequently used to describe the considerable loss of species during the "pre-taxonomic" period, roughly between 1500s and 1800s, as well as, to a lesser extent, during the "taxonomic period," from 1800s to the present. An anthropogenic extinction process was sparked by navigators' discovery of oceanic islands and other virgin environments and the subsequent introduction of destructive species like rats and goats. Before systematic scientific recording, the ecology underwent significant alteration.

From ancient times humans were a reason in animal extinction and decrease of animal population and in the 1800s, industrialization drove up extinction rates and has continued to do so. Among many species which are currently endangered by pollutions, dams, other industrial pressures, poaching for food and accessories and other trades there are few species of animals which have been wiped off the face of earth.

Giant Ground Sloths

Up to the end of the last Ice Age, 2.5 million years ago, giant ground sloths were exclusively found in South America. One of the largest terrestrial creatures to ever exist, these sloths were enormous. They resembled elephants in size. They were herbivores that consumed fruits and foliage that no other animal could get, and they most likely lacked hair. Many people think that humans hunted the gigantic ground sloth to extinction, along with many other large mammals during the end of the last Ice Age.

Sabre-tooth

Sabre-tooth Cats existed between 55 million and 11,700 years ago and were frequently dubbed as Sabre-toothed Tigers or Sabre-toothed Lions. The carnivorous Sabre-tooth Cats got their name from their long, blade-like canine teeth, which may reach 50 cm in certain species. They had a very bear-like build and were regarded as superb hunters, taking down prey like sloths and mammoths. These cats had jaws that could expand at an angle of 120 degrees, which is almost twice as wide as a lion of today! It is thought that the decline and extinction of the large herbivores that the sabre-tooth cat hunted may have contributed to their extinction. Competition with humans and climate change are two further factors.

Fig: Sabre-tooth

Woolly Mammoth

Woolly Mammoth is a massive creature that is thought to be linked to current day elephants. Its ancestors left Africa around 3.5 million years ago and dispersed across northern Eurasia and North America. It could weigh more than 6 tonnes and stood over 4 metres tall. Their curving tusks quickly reached a length of 5 metres, and they were clothed in fur. After being hunted by humans and having its habitat destroyed by climate change, the Woolly Mammoth eventually vanished 10,000 years ago. On Wrangel Island in the Arctic Ocean, the final isolated colony of woolly mammoths is thought to have perished approximately 1700 BC.

Fig: Woolly Mammoth

Moa

The moa was the only species of wingless bird known to have existed, and were found in New Zealand. In the woods of New Zealand, they were the predominant plant-eaters, and the Haast's Eagle was their sole predator. Despite nearly typically being portrayed as giants, several Moa species were actually much smaller than people, with some possibly of being as small as chickens. How the moa made it to the islands of New Zealand was a mystery because it was completely devoid of wings.

Moa were probably already present in New Zealand when it separated from the supercontinent of Gondwana some 80 million years ago. When humans first arrived in New Zealand between 1250s and 1300s, the moa became a ready source of food for the new immigrants. Humans hunted it for food, and habitat loss from deforestation and the introduction of invasive species also hurt it. In the 15th century, saw the final reported sighting of them.

Eurasian Aurochs

The Eurasian aurochs, a big wild ox that formerly roamed the steppes of Europe, Siberia, and Central Asia, is one of the ancestors of present-day cattle. They appeared in the bestiaries created by naturalists who may have really seen them. They were hunted by the Romans, who manufactured hunting horns out of their horns. Hunting undoubtedly contributed to their decrease, but domestication's primary and secondary consequences were equally significant.

As human civilization advanced, agriculture changed the aurochs' natural environment, and hunting and habitat loss sealed this wild bovine's demise. Its extinction marked the first time an animal's disappearance was recorded by humans. The last one, a female, was killed in what is now Poland in 1627.

Dodo

The dodo bird is one of the most famous examples of human-induced extinction. A large, flightless bird once native to the island of Mauritius in the Indian Ocean that was never inhabited or touched by humans until a few centuries ago. Dodos had no natural predators. Since as far as we know no other animals needed to eat Dodos or dodo eggs, but plants needed Dodos for pollination or seed dispersal, the extinction of Dodos by itself had an effect of the food web there.

Fig: Dodo

When humans came and started to settle there, it quickly decimated the dodo population as it was an easy source of fresh meat for their journeys. The birds were further threatened by habitat loss as people began to inhabit the island. Additionally, humans brought animals with them, including pigs and monkeys, which preyed on the dodos' vulnerable eggs and competed with them for food. The dodos were unable to survive due to poaching of the birds, habitat loss, and a losing battle with newly introduced animals. The last dodo was killed in 1681, and the species was lost forever to extinction.

Stellers Sea Cow

The Stellers Sea Cow was a sizable herbivorous animal that was named after the naturalist George Steller, who discovered it in 1741. The Near Islands, located southwest of Alaska, and the Commander Islands in the Bering Sea are thought to have been home to Stellers Sea Cows, which grew to at least 8-9 metres in length and weighed roughly 8-10 tonnes. The creature was thought to be domesticated and spent much of its time eating kelp; this, along with the possibility that it couldn't submerge its massive body, may have made it vulnerable to human hunters. After being found by humans, Steller's Sea Cow was hunted to extinction in about 27 years.

Great Auk

The North Atlantic was home to the flightless Great Auk, which spent much of its time in the cooler waters near Iceland, Greenland, and Canada. On their flanks they had a characteristic pattern of elevated rising buttons. They had webbed feet, a long tail, a long neck, a big head, and light brown fur. The Great Auk was a marine bird that swam and dove for food while submerged in the sea. Wherever there was protection from predators and easy access to the water, it chose to nest on rocky islands and coastal cliffs.

Fig: Great Auk

The Great Auk was a carnivorous bird that consumed small marine creatures like fish and crustaceans. It could hold its breath for up to a minute and descend to depths of more than 100 feet, making it a skilled swimmer and diver. Due to a mixture of human activities, such as hunting, collecting eggs, and habitat loss, the Great Auk is now extinct. Local settlers and fishermen engaged in widespread hunting of the bird since it was highly sought for its meat, feathers, and oil. The Great Auk was officially declared extinct in 1852 after the last recorded pair was slain by hunters on the Icelandic Island of Eldey in 1844.

Labrador Duck

The last time a Labrador duck was spotted in North America was in Elmira, New York, in 1878. The species' females have grey feathers, while the males had black and white ones. They possessed long bills, small eyes, and small heads. The tail was rounded, and the body was short. Although it moved over the winter, it chose Labrador's coasts to be where it bred. The Labrador duck was never common, but it is thought that hunting and probably egg gathering contributed to its extinction. The disappearance of food sources and the displacement of the duck from its habitat have both been suggested as potential causes of its extinction.

Quagga

The quagga has a zebra-horse hybrid appearance. It is a subspecies of plains zebras and is closely related to South African zebra kind whose stripes dwindled below the neck. According to researchers who have studied zebras' DNA, the quagga is a subspecies of the plains zebra rather than what was once believed to be a different species. They were valuable for their meat and hides but also for its tongue, which was considered a delicacy, and people wanted to preserve the vegetation quaggas fed on for domesticated livestock. Many creatures were wiped off by widespread hunting in South Africa in the 1800s, and quaggas were driven to extinction. On August 12, 1883, the last quagga to be alive passed away in a zoo in Amsterdam.

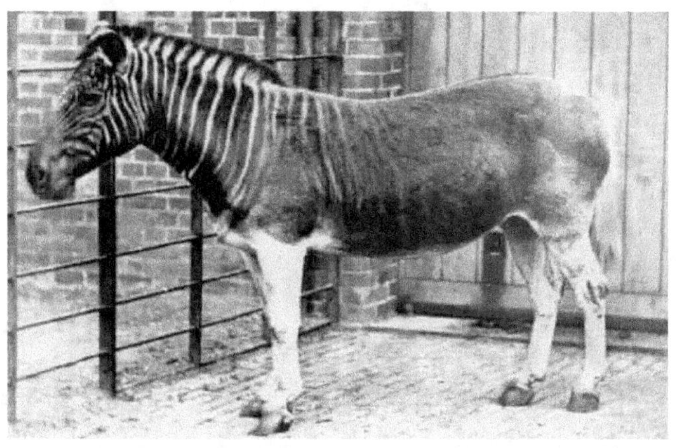

Fig: Quagga

These are few animal species that were pushed to extinction by humans in one way or the other and that too at the earlier stages of industrialization. There may be many more species which may have become extinct but due to lack of records of them or due to missing pieces of their stories in the history, may have led to their unrecognisable conditions. But with current technology slowly we are able to recover the remains and discover many species which went extinct that we don't even know.

3.19th century

Large number of animal species went extinct since 19th century due to modernization and development of technology, which led to modern approaches for hunting, trading and many more fields which utilized animals as their main product for the development and functioning. Animal trades for exhibitions, or materials like fur or other parts which were utilized for creation of various materials, which increased hunting them and pushed most of the species to extinction.

Since 1970 alone, 133 species have been lost, from ants, bees, beetles, butterflies and dragonflies, to fish, fleas, fungi, mammals, moths, shrimps, spiders and wasps. Freshwater species populations declined by more than 80% between 1970 and 2012, mostly due to habitat loss from dams and water abstraction. The amount of life in the seas declined by a third over the same period, mostly due to overfishing.

Other reason is due to deforestation for agriculture and expansion of cities and villages for human settlements which decreased the habitats of animals. Loss of habitat can also lead to increased encounters between wild species and people. People may become more exposed to wild species as development pushes them farther into a species' range. Closer to homes and schools may grow poisonous plants and fungus. Additionally, wild creatures are seen more regularly.

These animals are merely patrolling their territory, but coming into contact with humans can be fatal. Predators that lose their habitat to buildings, farms, and commercial establishments include polar bears, mountain lions, and alligators. Native species could become endangered as a result of people killing natural animals through pesticides, accidents like collisions with cars, or hunting.

The number of species that went extinct due to various reasons and situations caused by humans is large. They are many which once existed in large numbers but due to overhunting or due to loss of their natural habitat or due to other reasons, they went extinct in no time.

Passenger Pigeon

The passenger pigeon, has been gone from the earth for more than a century. This bird species was once found in large numbers soaring over North American skies and while it was considered among the most populous birds, it is now extinct. Estimates say that the passenger pigeon population numbered in the millions and possibly billions till 1800s. The Passenger Pigeon was a major food source for many indigenous peoples and was hunted for its feathers and meat. The human-induced hunting of passenger pigeons significantly slowed the species' population, leading to their mass extinction. The exact last bird known with certainty died in 1914.

Fig: Passenger Pigeon

Carolina Parakeet

Carolina Parakeet was found in old forests along rivers in the eastern United States, from southern New York and Wisconsin all the way to the Gulf of Mexico. The feathers of this parrot species were magnificent. The vibrant feathers of this species of parrot have contribute only to their demise.

The Carolina Parakeet, the sole parrot endemic to the Eastern United States, has bright feathers in a range of hues, including green, yellow, and red and they were widely valued as hat decorations for women. As a result, more people were hunting and killing this endangered species, which causes its numbers to decline. The Cincinnati Zoological Garden's Lady Jane and Incas, the last two captive Carolina parakeets, perished in 1918, effectively putting an end to the species.

Sicilian Wolf

The Sicilian Wolf population, which was once present in Sicily, is one of the indigenous grey wolves. Significant population decreases have been seen in a number of local grey wolf packs over the years. For a variety of reasons, such as losing their habitat, some species have even become extinct. On the largest island in the Mediterranean Sea, this wolf species once flourished before it was eradicated and eventually went extinct.

The Sicilian Wolf has gone extinct as a result of human activity. A study claims that people are to blame for the wolf's extinction because of their insatiable desire for farmer's animals. Additionally, it is thought that the island's environmental crisis and natural calamities led to the population reduction. They eventually vanished from the island around 1920s.

Paradise Parrot

The paradise parrot is at the top of our list of extinct animals in the past century. This animal no longer lives or exists anywhere in the world. The species was once observed wandering through eucalyptus forests in river valleys of eastern Australia. The Paradise parrot is a little bird with a length of 27 to 30 inches. This amazing bird has a long tail and a red scapular. A male Paradise parrot has an ebony crown and a bright red forehead. Sadly, since 1928, it has not been seen. Severe drought, predator activity, habitat degradation, eucalyptus tree cutting, and overgrazing of farm animals are a few reasons for their extinction.

Heath Hen

Heath hen was once abundant along the east coast of the United States, which is now extinct. Only found on Martha's Vineyard in the United States, it is a smaller subspecies of the larger prairie chicken. The Heath hen is thought to have vanished within the last century due to a variety of factors. Its numbers have decreased mostly as a result of wildfires, poaching, and habitat changes.

Fig: Heath Hen

In their natural environment during colonial times, Heath Hens were quite common. However, since they were gallinaceous birds, settlers hunted them extensively to augment their food supply. After the last known heath hen died, the species was officially declared extinct in 1933.

Desert Rat-kangaroo

The desert rat-kangaroo, a little jumping marsupial, has been extinct for the past 100 years. The Central Australian deserts are home to this kangaroo, sometimes known as the plains rat kangaroo or the buff-nosed rat kangaroo.

Although it looks like a kangaroo, the desert rat-kangaroo actually has the bulk of a small rabbit. In contrast to kangaroos, it has a blunt, short and wide skull, rounded short ears, and an exposed nose. Its natural habitat was extremely arid, and it spends more time at night. In the eastern Lake Eyre basin of northern south Australia, the last reported sighting occurred in 1935.

Tasmanian Tiger

The Tasmanian Tiger, often referred to as the Tasmanian Wolf and Thylacine, had interesting characteristics, its back has 15 to 20 prominent dark stripes that could be seen from the shoulders to the tail. The Tasmanian Tiger was also referred to as a vampire dog in the twentieth century due to its zebra-like stripes and canine-like form.

This amazing creature was native throughout the entire vast continent of Australia, including the islands of Tasmania and the nation of New Guinea. Thylacine was most active around dawn and late at night and it mostly hunted at night, either by itself or in pairs. The majority of its diet consisted of birds, smaller animals, and kangaroos.

Fig: Tasmanian Tiger

Due to their concern that the Tasmanian tiger might prey on their sheep, European colonists and farmers hunted it down and disease was also a caused which wiped out its numbers. The Tasmanian Tiger species perished as a result of this. The last known Tasmanian tiger died in Tasmania's Hobart Zoo in 1936.

Xerces Blue Butterfly

The Xerces blue butterflies lived in the coastal sand dunes of the San Francisco Peninsula. It was a type of tiny butterfly that was once discovered in coastal California in the US. The butterfly was originally widespread from San Francisco to California's coast, but due to habitat loss and pollution, its population started to fall in the early 1900s.

The coastal buckwheat plant was essential to the survival of the Xerces blue butterfly, which inhabited coastal meadows and dunes. Buckwheat was where the butterfly placed her eggs, and the plant's leaves were what the caterpillars ate.

Climate change and pesticides may have played a role in the butterfly's decline. The destruction and loss of its habitat is largely to blame for its demise. The Xerces blue butterfly was the first species of American butterfly to become extinct, and it was last seen around 1940s.

Japanese Sea Lion

Large creatures were abundant in the Pacific Ocean, including the Japanese sea lion, which used to swim freely in the sea and linger along bays in the Japanese Archipelago and on the Korean Peninsula. They are the only species of seals that can be found in both the northern and southern hemispheres and were the largest members of the Sea Lion family.

Sadly, it is one of the extinct species that can only be found in books, museums, and folklore but not in water. Japanese sea lions are thought to have walked freely along the shore until the 19th century, but they were last observed in the 1950s.

Only humans, who hunted them for their skins, whiskers, and internal organs, were the species' natural foes. Aside from being abducted, Japanese sea lions were also sold to circuses. In addition, it was targeted for harvesting and hunted because of fishing. This most certainly led to their extinction, along with discrimination from fishermen and even shooting by soldiers.

Crescent Nail Tail Wallaby

The Crescent nail tail wallaby was a small species of marsupial, one of the three known species of the genus, named for their distinctive tails with a claw or nail-like tip. The creature was comparable to a rabbit or hare in terms of look, behaviour, and taste. The species was timid and hid from humans. It grazed on grass in the woodlands and scrubs of Central and Southwestern Australia. The species' names were derived from their outward appearance, which included moon-like or pale crescent marks. The mark had light and dark patches of fur all over the body and goes from the shoulder behind the arm, around the flank, and finishes at a place directly above the thigh.

It had rather nice facial stripes, ashen grey fur that was soft and silky, and a colour that was partly reddish brown. It also had a horny spur at the end of its tail. Damage to their habitat and preying of foxes and cats introduced by humans have contributed to their extinction in the 1950s.

St. Helena Darter

St. Helena Darter is a species of dragonfly belongs to the Libellulidae family that was found only in St. Helena, a volcanic island in the Atlantic. There are a variety of factors that have contributed to this dragonfly's extinction. Although there were no direct dangers to this insect, the destruction of its environment is most likely the biggest threat to its existence. Its disappearance was also influenced by new invasive species that humans brought, such the African clawed frog. The last recorded sighting of the St. Helena Darter dragonfly occurred in 1963, thus ending its existence.

Mexican Brown Grizzlies

Similar to their siblings, these Mexican brown grizzlies were smaller than the brown bears found in the northern United States and Canada. Native Americans referred to them as "silver bears" because of their coloration, which ranged from a light buff-yellow to a grizzled grey or white that appeared silver in direct sunshine. The Mexican grizzly bear was an omnivore like other brown bears, consuming vegetation, fruits, insects, small mammals, and carrion. Cow farmers began to view the bears as pests as cow farming spread over the Mexican brown bear's territory, so they began to capture, shoot, and poison the animals. They were nearly exterminated by ranchers' hunting. They were last observed around 1964.

Fig: Mexican Brown Grizzlies

Guam Flying Fox

Guam is a tropical island in the Pacific Ocean, namely the tropical islands of the Marianas, which include Guam. It was home to the tiny Marianas fruit bat known as Guam flying fox. The extinction of this species of flying fox was largely caused by humans. Hunting as well as habitat encroachment contribute to this. Humans' food hunts for the Guam flying fox and their introduction of the venomous Brown tree snake both contributed to its extinction. Since 1968, since the last of these tiny fruit bats were hunted by hunters, no more have been seen.

Caspian Tiger

The Caspian Tiger was a magnificent tiger that was one of the largest big cats on the planet emphasizing the animal's immense size even further and used it to inhabit the lands of eastern Turkey, the Caspian Sea, and northern Iran. More than 10,000 years ago, these fierce tigers migrated from eastern China to the Caspian Sea, paving the way for the trade route that became to known as Silk Road. It is one of many well-known tigers, along with the Persian and Turan.

The Caspian tiger was unique, unlike all tigers, its legs were enormous. Although it had the distinctive tiger stripes, its true colour was quite distinct from that of other tiger species. Due to Russian colonial soldiers hunting it and people clearing land for farming, its population started declining in the late nineteenth century. The last Caspian tiger was believed to have been sighted in Turkey in 1970.

Round Island Burrowing Boa

The Round Island Burrowing Boa is a species of snake that has been extinct for the past many years and was last observed in 1975. The Round Island Burrowing Boa is a native of Round Island, a small island off the coast of Mauritius, and prefers to reside on the topsoil layers of volcanic slopes. It used to live on a number of different islands around Mauritius, but after the 1940s, when its population had drastically decreased, it could only be found on Round Island.

This snake, which is native to Round island in Mauritius, was around 1 meter in length overall, including the tail. Its colour is light brown with blackish dots and it has pink marbling on the ventral side. Its body and head are both cylindrical, and its snout is pointed. Despite not having a specific diet, it is assumed that it fed on lizards and their eggs. Additionally, it was believed to consume the eggs and chicks of seabirds that burrow and nest on the ground.

The primary contributing factor is the habitat loss brought on by soil erosion from excessive goat and rabbit grazing which pushed this species to extinct.

Yunnan Lake Newt

The Yunnan Lake newt is an extinct species of newt in the family Salamandridae, and was also known as Wolterstorff's newt. It was only discovered in Yunnan, China, close to Kunming Lake. It was discovered in nearby freshwater habitats and shallow lake waters. They consume the eggs and larvae of other amphibian species, as well as spiders, insects, worms, molluscs, crustaceans, and spiders.

The Yunnan Lake newt became extinct as a result of pollution, human-caused land reclamation from lake areas, duck farming, and the introduction of foreign fish and frog species to Kunming Lake in China. Since 1979, there have been no reports of it, hence it is now thought to be extinct.

Golden Toad

The Golden toad once lived in a great population in Costa Rica's Monteverde Cloud Forest. It was a notable frog with a striking burnt-yellow coloured skin that was nearly equivalent to gold, hence its name. The beautiful gold colour of these frogs must have been magnificent to see. The species spent the majority of its time underground, coming to the surface only occasionally to reproduce.

Chytridiomycosis, a fatal skin condition and infectious disease that kills frogs, is thought to be one of the causes of extinction. Additionally, as a result of global warming, a small population, and a lack of suitable habitat, the species' numbers have been steadily declined. The golden toad was last seen in 1989 in a Costa Rican rainforest before being declared extinct in 1994.

Fig: Golden Toad

Ivory-billed Woodpecker

The Ivory-billed woodpecker is a very large, extremely rare and extinct member of the woodpecker family. They were once common in the South American swamplands, but haven't been spotted since the 1940s. In rare cases, reports of hearing their characteristic pecking sound have been made instead of actual visual sightings.

The bird's neck and both the top and lower trailing edges of its wings are heavily marked with white. It is a glossy blue-black colour. It features a bill that is entirely white and a large upper crest that is either red or black depending on the gender. It is well known that ivory-billed storks favour dense hardwood swamps and pine woods with lots of dead and decaying trees.

Fig: Ivory-billed Woodpecker

The ivory-billed Woodpecker consumes a variety of foods, but primarily the larvae of wood-boring beetles. To find the insects, the bird peels, wedges, and hammers the bark off of dead trees with its large white bill. They were officially declared extinct in 1994.

Javan Tiger

The Javan tiger, which originated on the Indonesian island of Java, shared similarities in appearance with the Sumatran tiger. They were so prevalent on the island in the 1800s that locals thought of them as pests, but as the island grew, their numbers decreased. Due to the expansion of the agricultural business, they lost their habitat. They didn't die out from hunger or lack of reproduction, they were hunted. The last known tiger was slain in 1984, and ten years later, in 1994, they were officially declared extinct.

Fig: Javan Tiger

Bubal Hartebeest

The Bubal hartebeest was overhunted for many years, possibly centuries by humans, which ultimately led to its extinction. They are said to have appeared in ancient Egyptian tomb art and lived in the grasslands of North Africa until the 1950s. The northernmost areas of the Sahara Desert are where this fascinating species was last spotted in the wild.

The body of the Bubal hartebeest was said to be continuously sand coloured. It can be identified by the unique greyish patch that it has over each nostril on each side of its muzzle. Its horns were fashioned like a U and its shoulder measured 43 inches when viewed from the front.

Fig: Bubal Hartebeest

These hartebeest subspecies went extinct around 1950s, largely as a result of excessive human hunting. This species saw a severe decline over the nineteenth century, especially in the 19th century and eventually got extinct around 1994.

By the end of 19th century with or without realization many animal species met their demise or were in the stage near to extinction. Taking necessary measures to preserve these species was considered only after we lost many species and subspecies. Even after continuous measure to preserve these endangered species the poachers were running after their personal gain and continued hunting the last numbers of few species, for their parts which pushed most of the endangered species to extinction.

4.Current Day

Many animals were living peacefully on this Earth, except our human species, very long before we were evolved. They didn't collapse the system, but we humans have collapsed all possible nature's system in just few hundred years. There has never been a time in history when species extinction was as rapid. The last 200 years, Mother Earth saw many species suffer due to the so-called advancements did by us, humans, which caused the extinction of many species.

Due to habitat loss, excessive hunting, toxic pollution, new species invasion, and climate change, wildlife is dwindling. However, the experts assert that "human overpopulation and continued population growth, as well as overconsumption, especially by the rich," are the root causes of all of these issues.

The majority of documented extinctions have been on small islands, where species with small gene pools have usually succumbed to human hunters. That may be an ecological tragedy for the islands concerned, but most species live in continental areas and, ecologists agree that they are unlikely to prove so vulnerable.

When humans wipe out entire populations and species of other animals, they are chopping off the limb on which they rest and obliterating functional components of our own life-support system. The environment we live in gradually falls apart as a species goes extinct. The effects are severe, not only for those areas and those species, but also for all of us. These losses include both spiritual and cultural ones, as well as actual consequential losses like agricultural pollination and water purification.

The researchers discovered that up to 50% of all individual animals had disappeared in recent decades, and that a third of the hundreds of species losing populations are now categorised as endangered. Land mammals have detailed data, and nearly half of them have experienced an 80% loss in range during the past century. It has been discovered in a research that many communities of mammals, birds, reptiles, and amphibians have vanished from the world.

The species which went nearly extinct but due to our realization before their extinction made those to be preserved in wild life preservation centres. In 19th century many of the species went extinct and many were critically endangered due to us, but as some endangered species were saved and preserved, which helped them to regain their population and strive to live on. But few species even after several measures ultimately met their demise and went extinct due to various reasons from habitat and climatic change to lack of adaptability and survivability.

Sea Mink

The carnivorous sea mink, swam along the rocky coasts of New England and Nova Scotia. Due to the fact that sea minks were only discovered after going extinct, less is known about them. It was sought for as a product of the local fur trade, which eventually led to their demise. Some suggest that the sea mink was actually a subspecies of the American mink, it's closest living relative. Only after it had already been hunted to extinction in the late 19th or early 20th century more information about it came into light.

Pyrenean Ibex

The Pyrenees mountains, which run between Spain and France, as well as the mountains in northern Asia and Africa, are home to a variety of goat known as the Pyrenean ibex. The Pyrenees Ibex had long, unkempt, brown or grey hair and was the biggest goat in the entire globe. They were driven to extinction in the mid-19th century by trapping and poisoning across the Iberian Peninsula and southern France, but the species was declared extinct in 2000.

Fig: Pyrenean Ibex

Baiji White Dolphin

Another species that future generations will not have the pleasure of encountering is the baiji white dolphin, also referred to as the Chinese river dolphin. It was discovered in China's Yangtze River and was given the status of functionally extinct. Baiji are also known as killer whales, likely due to their enormous size and the fact that they could be distinguished by their long beaks and light grey skin.

The species is the only one known to pursue huge fish, including sharks, salmon, and bluefin tuna. With highly specialised organs, their bodies were designed for rapid swimming and effective oxygen uptake from water. They lived off fish and had weak vision, so they used sound to guide them through their hazy surroundings instead of sight.

Due to the construction of dams and other man-made buildings that restricted their movement and disturbed their natural environment, the baiji white dolphin population started to fall. Another aspect that contributed to its downfall was pollution from factories and boats. The last known baiji white dolphin died in 2002 and presumed extinct.

West African Black Rhino

An estimate says that one million rhinoceroses from four different species may have roamed the African savanna at the turn of the twentieth century. The other subspecies of rhinoceros that went extinct were genetically distinct from this rhinoceros. In the past, it was common in sub-Saharan Africa's savanna, where black rhinos of Western Africa browsed. In other words, they were herbivores who dined on morning and evening shoots and green vegetation. They writhed or slept off to snooze during the hottest hours of the day.

Early in the century, rhino numbers were quickly destroyed by widespread sports shooting. Then came industrial agriculture, which converted numerous former rhino habitats into farms and communities. The West African Black rhinoceros' fast population decline, which was caused by a number of factors including habitat degradation and poaching, which was formerly the most widespread big land animal on the African continent.

It was done to remove its horns which were believed to have medicinal value and to make ceremonial knife handles and for traditional Chinese medicine. The majestic West African black rhino was declared extinct in 2006, after conservationists failed to find any in their last remaining habitat in Cameroon.

Fig: West African Black Rhino

Madeiran Large White butterfly

The stunning Madeiran large white butterfly was found in the valleys of the Laurisilva forests on Portugal's Madeira Islands. This beautiful, delicate butterfly has the distinction of being declared for becoming the first insect in Europe to be declared extinct due to human activity. It was classified as extinct in 2007, because of habitat loss that was brought on by development and exposure to agricultural pesticides.

Fig: Madeiran Large White butterfly

Caribbean Monk Seal

The Caribbean Monk Seal is also known as the sea wolf or the West Indian seal. The Caribbean monk seal, the sole species of native seal to the region, is the first of the seal species to go extinct as a result of human activities. Its face had upward-opening nostrils, relatively large wide-spaced eyes, and fairly big whisker pads with long, smooth, and light-coloured whiskers.

Humans and sharks were their main predators. The two main factors contributing to the extinction of these seals are overfishing for food and overhunting for oils. They also suffered from starvation and eventually perished as a result of the destruction of the reefs, on which they relied for food. In addition to using the seals' fat as fuel, human colonists used them as food.

The reduction in seal populations was also a result of early scientists capturing the animals for research. The Caribbean monk seal went extinct in 2008 when its last colony was discovered on a remote coral off a tiny uninhabited Caribbean Island.

Siamese Flat-barbelled Catfish

The Siamese flat-barbelled catfish was a victim of humans building on land and rivers until its last sighting between 1975 and 1977. The Chao Phraya and Bang Pakong rivers in Thailand are where it reportedly originated. Lower to medium reaches, mainstreams, tributaries, and bigger marshlands were all occupied by it. It was a carnivore that consumed prawns and insects.

Its extinction is assumed to have been brought about by damming, canal construction, excessive river pollution, draining of wetlands in and around Bangkok, the capital of Thailand. In 2011, the species was deemed extinct.

Pinta Island Tortoise

The Pinta Island tortoise was around since Darwin's time and partially inspiring him in theory of evolution when he visited the Galapagos Islands in 1835. Fishermen continued to hunt the dwindling population throughout the twentieth century. The main cause of its widespread extinction was hunting. Whalers used this giant Island tortoise as food.

The Pinta Island tortoise was herbivore that consumed local plants like cactus pads, grasses, and fruits. They drank a lot of water, which their bodies then stored for later use. When it was time to sleep, it would do so for roughly 16 hours each day. The habitat of the tortoises was devastated by goats that humans introduced to Pinta in 1959.

Fig: Pinta Island Tortoise

Since they distributed seeds through herbivory and nutrient cycling, these species were crucial to the Island environment. As a result, as their population decreased, so did the island's ecosystem's capacity to function. This species was formally declared extinct in 2012 after the death of that last male in Galapagos National Park.

Northern White Rhino

The end of an evolutionary rope that reached back millions of years was Sudan, the last male northern white rhinoceros to ever roam the planet. His passing was a tragedy but it was expected. It was the grim climax of a conservation catastrophe that had been building for many years, exactly to this point. Sudan was the final male, yet he was not the last of his kind.

Two female descendants, Najin, a daughter, and Fatu, a granddaughter, were still alive and well. These two were grazing in an adjacent field while Sudan retreated. Their subspecies had become extinct. It could not be saved by two females acting alone. On March 19, 2018, the vets put him to sleep as he was on his last breaths.

Fig: Northern White Rhino (Najin & Fatu)

New Zealand Grayling

The New Zealand grayling is an extinct fish species that was native to New Zealand that migrated between fresh and saltwater habitats on New Zealand's coast. It was a stunning fish that had a silvery beginning, turned brown with a lighter belly over time, and occasionally went gold. It was a fish of medium size, reaching a length of about 30 to 45 centimetres.

Hundreds of New Zealanders hunted the fish at once. Early in the 1900s, there was a sharp fall in population. A New Zealand grayling was last seen in 1923. It was far too late to save the species when it was given protection in 1951, and it was formally deemed extinct in 2018.

Spix's Macaw

Brazil's unique Spix's macaw was last observed in the wild in 2016. This bird is also referred to as "Little Blue Macaw" because they're known for their vibrant blue feathers. German naturalist Johann Baptist von Spix discovered it in the interior of Brazil around 200 years ago. This species had its moment in the spotlight when one named Blu starred in the 2011 animated movie "Rio."

Unfortunately, habitat destruction and the illegal pet trade both played a significant role in the bird's extinction in the wild. Captive breeding programmes that aim to restore the birds to the wild offered hope for the survival of the species. It was declared extinct in the wild in 2019.

Smooth Handfish

The Smooth Handfish was a large, slow, and silvery fish which existed in abundance in the waters around Australia, in the Arctic Ocean and in the Bering Sea, just 200 years ago. The smooth handfish, so named because of its remarkable similarity to human arms and hands, also had a spike on its head that looked a lot like a punk-rock mohawk. Scientists believe that habitat degradation, net fishing, a shortage of food for them, and damaging fishing of other marine creatures are the likely causes of their extinction. This fish was officially declared as extinct in year 2020.

Fig: Smooth Handfish

Till current day the extinction of few species has been avoided but precautionary measures which safeguarded them from external factors like environmental changes, habitat changes, and mainly hunters. Some species showed great improvement in their population and got adapted to the new habitats and strived further. But few species are still struggling to maintain their numbers. More care is taken for such animals and helping them in breeding and adapting so that they will not go extinct.

But even after so much care, some cases are realized late, as a result, even after many necessary precautions and safeguard measures some species of animals are still going towards extinction and few are already extinct. Like the northern white rhino few species are moving towards extinction and even after many measures, they are not working effectively to revive the species resulting in extinction.

5.Endangered species

Endangered means to be under threat or near extinction. There are many endangered species in the globe. When a species or animal is in risk of extinction or has a very tiny population that is insufficient to ensure its survival, it is considered to be endangered. Many of those species are in danger of going extinct as a result of human interference for food or amusement. These animals are endangered for a variety of causes, including the demand for their fur, the oil they produce, and their use as food.

Any species that is threatened with extinction due to a sharp decline in population or the loss of a vital habitat is considered an endangered species. Hot spots are biodiverse areas that need to be protected because they house a large number of endangered species. Previously, any plant or animal species that faced extinction may be referred to as an endangered species.

The requirement for distinct definitions of "endangered" and "threatened" species led to the creation of a number of classification schemes, each of which contains definitions and standards by which a species might be categorised according to its risk of extinction. Before a species can be categorised, a variety of factors must often be examined.

Among the species threatened with extinction are rhinos and eagles. The researchers say that losing these creatures will bring about the collapse of ecosystems on which humans depend for food and water. Because they take longer to grow up and reproduce than smaller birds and animals, larger animals are at greater risk and also, they find it difficult to change their diet or environment. Therefore, they simply do not have enough time to adjust to a world that is changing rapidly.

According to the International Union for Conservation of Nature (IUCN), hundreds of marine species across the world come under endangered and critically endangered categories. Numerous marine species, such as the North Atlantic Right Whale, Whale Sharks, Asian Giant Softshell Turtle found in Southeast Asia, porpoises, bluefin tuna, sea otters, manatees, and fur seals, are on the verge of extinction as a result of climate change, habitat loss, and overfishing, which pose a serious threat to their survival.

The International Union for Conservation of Nature (IUCN) maintains a "Red List of Threatened Species." The seriousness and precise root causes of an endangered species' endangerment are outlined in the Red List. The Red List has seven levels of conservation: least concern, near threatened, vulnerable, endangered, critically endangered, extinct in the wild, and extinct. Each category represents a different threat level.

Species that are not threatened by extinction are placed within the first two categories—least concern and near-threatened. Those that are most threatened are placed within the next three categories, known as the threatened categories—vulnerable, endangered, and critically endangered. Those species that are extinct in some forms are placed within the last two categories—extinct in the wild and extinct.

Blue Whale

The largest living animal on earth, the blue whale, belongs to the baleen whales and features more than 100 feet in length and around 200 tonnes in weight. There are currently five subspecies of blue whales, and they can be seen travelling in the oceans around the world from both polar regions. With the exception of the Arctic Ocean, blue whales can be found in every ocean.

As the top of the food chain, whales play a crucial part in preserving the marine ecosystem. Sadly, despite a global prohibition being established in 1966, excessive commercial hunting has significantly reduced its number and is now endangering its very existence. Whales are hunted and killed for their marketable parts, such as their meat and blubber, which may be processed into a particular form of oil. In 1970, blue whales were declared endangered.

Fig: Blue Whale

Fin Whale

The second-largest animal on the earth, after the blue whale, is the fin whale, also referred to as the common rorqual. The fin whale has a maximum length of 25.9 metres and is thought to weigh over 114 tonnes. The fin whale suffers from hunting just like every other whale in our oceans does.

Humpback Whale

Another rorqual species, the humpback whale, has been classified as an endangered marine species. As a result of hunting for their skin and meat, this species' population decreased by 90%. There are only about 2,500 humpback whales left in existence.

Grey Whale

Grey whales are remarkable among whales for having dorsal humps in place of fins. These 50-foot whales are known for their moans, growls, knocks, and other peculiar vocalisations. While grey whales in the Baja California area are generally regarded as gentle, the species is infamous for how fiercely mothers guard their new-borns.

Due to centuries of overfishing, the Western North Pacific and North Atlantic populations are now critically threatened. The good news is that due to fishing limitations, the third population in the Eastern North Pacific was able to recover to the point that it was taken off the U.S. Endangered Species List.

Right Whale

Right whales have been hunted since the 11th century, and in 1935 they were finally protected from whaling. Even so, despite growing risks from climate change, vessel collisions, and unintentional entanglement in fishing gear, the population has had a difficult time recovering. Right whales were protected from these threats by implementing a dedicated efforts to rescue this endangered species.

Research shows that whales act as ecosystem engineers and supply phytoplankton, tiny ocean plants that produce at least 50% of our oxygen, hundreds of thousands of tonnes of carbon annually, and a base for the marine food web leading to abundant fish stocks, with the nutrients they desperately need. It is anticipated that fewer than 350 right whales are left in current day.

Fig: Right Whale

Bison

Bison were central in the lives and traditions of many Native nations and an umbrella species for many plants and animals sharing its habitat. The United States' Great Plains were home to millions of bison before the 1800s, but by the late 1880s, they were all but extinct. For the price of their hides, bison were slain in unbelievable large numbers. Additionally, they were hunted to ease railroad congestion and take away an important Native American food supply.

Because the roots of the grasses are rich in vitamins and minerals to promote rapid regrowth, the vegetation on the Plains was well adapted to the diet of the bison. The demand for buffalo skin soared around the start of the 19th century in North America, Europe, and Canada. Thousands of them were hunted across the Great Plains, and by 1890, their number had fallen from 30 million to just over 1,000.

Fig: Bison

Although their numbers shrank to a perilously small figure at the end of the 19th century due to overhunting, bison weren't federally classified as an endangered species in the United States. Public bison preservation efforts began in 1907 when 15 were relocated to New York's Bronx Zoo. The Intertribal Bison Cooperative was founded by South Dakotan tribes in 1990, and it now has 57 member tribes that look after 15,000 bison.

Amur Leopard

While most people associate leopards with the African savannas, a rare subspecies of the species has adapted to living in the temperate forests that make up the northernmost portion of the species' habitat in the Russian Far East. The Amur leopard can run up to 37 kilometres per hour, just like other leopards can. The Amur leopard lives by himself. It is swift on its feet and strong, carrying and hiding incomplete kills to prevent other predators from stealing them. With only around 80 – 90 are remaining in the wild, the Amur leopard is one of the most endangered big cats in the world.

These leopard subspecies have been listed as severely endangered since 1996, despite the fact that their wild population appears to be stable and growing. Around 75% of their home range lies in protected areas in Russia and China, and they are also moving into suitable habitats outside of these protected areas.

Poachers kill them for their coats and bones, the latter of which is sold for use in conventional Asian medicine, making them incredibly susceptible to such attacks. Due to both natural and artificial fires, they are vulnerable to habitat loss. The availability of prey is also declining as a result of climate change are leading them to endangerment.

African Forest Elephant

The elusive relative of the African savanna elephant is the African forest elephant. They live in the tropical woods of central and western Africa. Since they favour deep forest environment, conventional counting techniques like visual identification are impossible. "Dung counts" an examination of the density and distribution of the faeces on the ground are typically used to estimate their population.

While some African elephant populations are growing, especially in southern Africa, numbers are still declining in other regions, particularly in central Africa and some regions of East Africa. The other species of African elephant, the African savanna elephant, is smaller than the African forest elephant. African forest elephants feed on leaves, grasses, seeds, fruit, and tree bark. They can live in family groups of up to 20 elephants.

Fig: African Forest Elephant

Forest elephants are essential for spreading many different tree species' seeds, especially those of huge trees with a high carbon content because fruit makes up the majority of their diet. Savanna elephants reproduce significantly faster than forest elephants do, hence the latter cannot recover from population decreases as quickly.

Saola

Often called the Asian unicorn, the saola is one of the rarest mammals on the planet. The Annamite Range in Vietnam was the site of its initial discovery in 1992, which was so fascinating that it was heralded as one of the most remarkable zoological discoveries of the 20th century. Saola is considered the Asian unicorn because it is so elusive and hardly seen. They are a cousin of cattle but resemble an antelope and have striking white markings on the face and large maxillary glands on the muzzle. It is one of the rarest large terrestrial mammals on Earth and is thought to be critically endangered, while precise population estimates are difficult to come by.

Mountain Gorilla

Gorillas come in two species—the Eastern and Western gorillas, each of which has two subspecies. A subspecies of the eastern gorilla known as the mountain gorilla, it is only found in two isolated populations in the high-altitude forests of the volcanic mountains of the Democratic Republic of the Congo, Rwanda, and Uganda, as well as in Uganda's Bwindi Impenetrable National Park. Gorillas are amazing animals that have 98.3% of our DNA in common. They are capable of experiencing emotions just like we do, and they occasionally even act like us.

Compared to other great apes, they have thicker fur. They can endure in a habitat where temperatures frequently drop below freezing thanks to their fur. People began to believe that they constitute a serious threat to their safety because of their violent behaviour. They began killing them, and even after numerous conservation efforts, their population is still not protected from poachers.

Fig: Mountain Gorilla

In 1989, there were only 620 mountain gorillas left, but since then, significant conservation initiatives have resulted in the population steadily growing again. With barely over 1,000 living in the wild, mountain gorillas are officially classified as an endangered species.

Orangutan

The name orangutan means "man of the forest" in the Malay language of Malaysia. Orangutans live alone in the lowland forests where they are found. They drink water from holes in trees and eat wild fruits like lychees, mangosteens, and figs. They build nests in the vegetation-covered trees where they spend the night and relax during the day. Although they may look more like melted Muppets than actual people morphologically, their highly developed cognitive capacities are in fact very human. They have been observed using tools, just like chimpanzees and gorillas.

Both the Bornean and the Sumatran orangutan species have seen dramatic decreases in their populations. Orangutans from Borneo and Sumatra have a few subtle behavioural and physical differences. Their primary threat comes from habitat loss brought on by deforestation for palm oil, which is driven by humans.

Pangolin

Pangolins are actually mammals, though many think of them as reptiles. They are the only mammals whose entire body is covered in scales, and they employ these scales as defence against predators in the wild. A pangolin will immediately curl into a tight ball and defend itself using its sharp-scaled tail if it feels threatened. Pangolins, also referred to as the scaly anteater, it devours termites, ants, and larvae. Pangolins consume with their long, sticky tongues, which can occasionally extend farther than the animal itself, as they lack teeth. They undoubtedly rank among the most heavily trafficked mammals in Asia and to a greater extent in Africa.

Fig: Pangolins

In nations like China and Vietnam, pangolins are in high demand. Scales from pangolins are utilised in traditional medicine and folk medicines, and their meat is prized as a delicacy. In 2016, a treaty of over 180 governments announced an agreement that would end all legal trade of pangolins and further protect the species from extinction.

Przewalski's

Inhabiting only certain areas in Central Asia such as the Gobi Desert and adjacent regions lies a subspecies of wild horses called Przewalski's or Mongolian wild horses' a holy animal of Mongolia. These animals remain few in number and are critically endangered. The Przewalski's horse, believed to have roamed the grasslands and desert of the Central Asian steppes for more than 160,000 years, however the captive population in Europe was barely hanging on after the two world wars.

Today, there are about 1,900 out of them, over 400 horses are roaming freely in the Mongolian steppes. This is a huge milestone for an endangered species heading toward extinction. Thanks to persistent conservation measures and effective reintroduction initiatives their numbers have slowly but surely risen. Nevertheless, it is crucial to acknowledge that they remain critically endangered.

Fig: Przewalski's

Javan Rhino

Rhinos are one of the most poached animals on the planet. Their horns are used in traditional Chinese medicine and displayed as a symbol and demonstration of wealth. The black rhino, the Javan rhino, and the Sumatran rhino are three of the five species of rhinos that are among the most endangered in 2022 as a result of poaching. Of these rhino species, the Javan Rhinoceros is one of the most endangered.

The Javan rhino shares striking physical similarities with the closely related larger one-horned rhinoceros, but differs in that it has a smaller skull and fewer noticeable skin folds. With only about 60 individuals remaining, all of which are in Indonesia's Ujung Kulon National Park, the Javan rhino is the species that is most in danger of going extinct. In contrast, the black rhino population is thought to number over 5,500.

Sahul Reef Snake

The short-nosed sea snake known as Sahul reef snake is a venomous snake endemic to the Ashmore Reef and Hibernia reefs on the north-western_Australian coastline. Its blunt face and length of up to 24 inches earned it the nickname short-nosed sea snake. While they could dive for up to two hours without taking a breath because their skin absorbed oxygen, they had to return to the ocean's surface to breathe. It's interesting to note that they shed their skin more frequently than land snakes to get rid of barnacles or other aquatic life that might adhere to them. They had increased epidermal surface area to absorb oxygen as a result.

They foraged on coral reefs and for eels and fish, but experts think warmer seas, trawlers, increased boat traffic, and water contamination caused their decline. For the last 23 years, the short-nosed sea snake was thought extinct at Ashmore Reef but now this lost species has been found by researchers during a deep-sea expedition, 67m below the ocean surface in the twilight zone.

Hawksbill Turtle

The population of the Hawksbill turtle has been appeared to have decreased by 80% over the past century. It is found in the tropical parts of all of the world's oceans, gulfs, and seas, mostly in coral reefs. The Hawksbill turtle is a valuable commodity on the market because of its colourful, beautifully patterned shell, which is frequently referred to as tortoiseshell are being sold. These turtles have been ruthlessly slaughtered for a considerable amount of time and are well known to be heavily trafficked in the tourist trade in tropical areas for their meat and shells.

Fig: Hawksbill Turtle

Although collecting its eggs is prohibited in many nations, the practise could not be completely stopped. The Hawksbill turtle primarily feeds on coral reef species, and the degradation of these species has also led to a decline in its population.

Kemp's Ridley Sea Turtle

The Kemp's Ridley Sea turtle, also known as the Atlantic Ridley Sea turtle, it is endangered as the rarest and smallest sea turtle. The Kemp's Ridley Sea turtle, which is mostly found in the Gulf of Mexico, frequently migrates to the Atlantic Ocean before returning to lay eggs. Oil spills, a shortage of food supply, marine pollution, and entanglement in fishing gear are all threats to sea turtles.

Sadly, the population of Kemp's Ridley Sea turtles has drastically decreased as a result of factors like habitat loss, marine pollution, entrapment in fishing nets, etc. To rescue this threatened marine species, research efforts have been started that involve incubation and hatching the eggs in temperature-controlled environments. Egg harvesting has also been made illegal in order to protect this species.

Green Sea Turtle

One of the largest sea turtles, the Green Sea Turtle, is herbivore and it is usually found in the tropical and subtropical seas and encountering a green sea turtle in the wild is a truly breath-taking experience. Without further efforts to save these huge herbivores, one that we would collectively encounter less and less. The green colour of the fat found behind the carapace of green sea turtles' shells, which results from the algae and sea grasses they eat, gives them their name. The search for turtles and their eggs threatens the lives of these sea turtles because they are a popular food.

Their number has declined as a result of the removal of sandy beaches and irresponsible fishing. The green turtle is a common resident of coastal regions around the world, but it also faces a number of dangers. Threats to it include unintentional catch in fishing gear, egg collection, habitat deterioration during nesting, vessel strikes, ocean pollution, a changing climate, and disease. There are numerous ways developed to help this endangered species of marine mammal, despite the numerous risks it confronts.

Smalltooth Sawfish

The odd-looking smalltooth sawfish could pass for a crocodile-shark hybrid with its cartilaginous body and elongated snout, but it's a species of ray. These migratory fish are found off the Florida coast and like warm tropical waters. The Gulf of Mexico, from Texas to Florida and up the East Coast to North Carolina, once included smalltooth sawfish in every area. The loss of habitat and accidental capture were the two main causes of the smalltooth sawfish population collapse in the second half of the 20th century.

The Florida coast's tiny estuaries, where young smalltooth sawfish loved to nurse, started to disappear as coastal development continued to soar. At the same time, fishermen were accidentally catching the fish in their nets, killing them rather than releasing them caused decline in their number.

Hammerhead Shark

The Hammerhead shark, a member of the Sphyrnidae family, is found in tropical oceans all over the world. It gets its name from its head's "hammer" shape. The shark can identify the direction of a scent and observe prey from above and below simultaneously because to its distinctive "hammer" shaped head. These sharks, who are renowned for being aggressive hunters, prey on smaller fish, squid, crustaceans, and octopuses.

There have also been stories of the sharks attacking people without warning. Hammerhead sharks have a lengthy lifespan, mature after a number of years, and produce few offspring, just like humans. It is thought that hammerheads have lost up to 80% of their original population. Due of their distinctive head shape, hammerhead sharks are particularly susceptible to getting captured in fishing nets. It is a fact that 370t of hammerhead sharks are legally permitted to be captured each year in Australian seas, commercial fishing poses the biggest threat to hammerheads.

Fig: Hammerhead Shark

Along with vessel strikes, bycatch in nets, and lethal shark control programmes, additional regional hazards like oil and gas drilling also pose a threat to hammerhead shark populations. One of the shark species that is most in risk of going extinct globally is the great hammerhead.

Mediterranean and Hawaiian Monk Seals

The Mediterranean Monk Seal, which previously stretched from Portugal to Senegal, one of many endangered species worldwide. Hawaiian Monk Seal, a native of the North-western Hawaiian Islands, is one of the earless seals that inhabit warm beaches, in contrast to other seals. Together with the Mediterranean monk seal, this species of marine animal is down to just two living individuals. The Caribbean monk seal, the third species in this genus, has already vanished from the globe.

These seals are threatened because to commercial hunting for meat, oil, and skin, attacks from predators like tiger sharks, marine debris, and entrapment in fishing nets, as well as habitat deterioration, pollution, the depletion of fisheries, and global warming.

Southern Sea Otters

Southern sea otters can live in frigid seas without the fat layer that protects other marine mammals because they have the world's thickest fur. They consume up to a fifth of their body weight each day in food, which is another requirement for keeping warm. Off the coast of California, less than 3,000 southern sea otters are present. As a result of the fur trade, sea otters faced their greatest threats in the past, when their population fell from over a million to less than 2,000. This species is endangered due to ongoing threats such as oil spills, habitat loss, food shortages, disease, entanglement in fishing gear, and competition with shellfish fisheries.

Hector's Dolphins

Found off the coast of New Zealand, Hector's Dolphins are the smallest dolphin in the world and the most prominent dolphin species. The world's rarest dolphins have stocky bodies, black patterns on their faces, and a creamy white throat and belly. They are typically seen in the South Island area. Hector's Dolphins typically come in groups of two to eight individuals.

Unfortunately, there is a significant decline in their population as trawl fisheries, and bottom-set gill nets a type of fishing nets cause the death of these species. The Hector's dolphin is a "red list" endangered species according to the International Union for Conservation of Nature, with only 7,400 individuals thought to be alive in the coastal seas off New Zealand.

Stellar Sea Lion

Stellar sea lion the largest member of the Otariid family and the fourth largest of all sea lion species. It may be found in the chilly North Pacific coast waters. The species bears Georg Wilhelm Steller's name, a naturalist who made the first discovery of them in 1741. This marine life is endangered because to the high risk of predation by killer whales, as well as fishing and harvesting by native Alaskans and Canadians for meat, oil, hides, and other products.

Since the 1960s, sources claim both natural and human dangers have caused its population to drop by more than 60%. In 2013, the eastern Steller sea lion population had seen a rise which reduced their endangerment.

Gharial

A crocodilian, the gharial has a scraggly (thin and bony) appearance. They are sometimes referred to as gavials, and their long, slender snouts make them simple to identify. Despite originally being prevalent from Pakistan to Myanmar, according to National Geographic, they are currently only found in India and Nepal. They flourish in freshwater ecosystems.

These animals have been put in danger by human hunting and environmental changes. The ability to obtain water is essential for gharials to thrive, therefore when something like a dam alters that availability, they may suffer as a result, making them an endangered species.

Fig: Gharial

Whale shark

Whale sharks are one of the big fishes alive today and the biggest shark in general. These organisms, despite their size, are filter feeders, which means they use their enormous mouths to consume plankton and other small fish. All of the world's tropical waters have whale sharks. These gentle giants can be easily identified by their white speckled colouring.

Fig: Whale Shark

Intentional fishing, accidental capture in nets, and vessel impacts are the greatest hazards to whale sharks, but there are other regional dangers like oil and gas extraction. These days, whale sharks are protected from fishing in many nations, yet their numbers are declining in many places.

With a fantastic success rate of 99% of the species listed on it, the Endangered Species Act (ESA) is most successful statute to protect at-risk species from extinction. Critical habitat areas must be protected, and recovery plans for listed species must be created and carried out. It also permits flexibility in how it is put into practise, calling for cooperation of extinction-prevention measures by federal, state, tribal, and local authorities.

To establish whether a particular species is making a comeback, populations are tracked over time. Species are taken off the list when they are deemed to have recovered. A species' gradual recovery calls for sustained effort and is influenced by a variety of factors, including habitat, food supply, reproduction rate, and climate. The longer a species remains listed, the more likely it is to be recovering.

The Endangered Species Act creates protections for fish, wildlife, and plants that are listed as threatened or endangered. It allows for the addition of species to the list of threatened and endangered species and the removal of those species from the list as well as the preparation and implementation of recovery plans. It also allows for interagency cooperation to prevent the taking of listed species and the issuance of permits for otherwise prohibited activities, it also allows for cooperation with States, including authorising certain activities.

When a species is declared endangered under the Endangered Species Act, it is forbidden to harass, injure, pursue, hunt, shoot, wound, kill, set traps, catch, or attempt to collect that species. The ESA's vulnerable species list may also include species that are subject to similar bans. Additionally, critical habitat must be set aside for the species' conservation.

Internationally, 199 countries have signed an accord to create Biodiversity Action Plans to address the conservation of threatened species and habitats. Many worthwhile organizations also exist to protect endangered species. On the verge of extinction, animals are sought out and saved, their health is restored, they can breed and raise their young safely, a sustainable habitat is created, and the habitat is protected from encroachment. This helps the endangered animals survive until their numbers are such that they have a chance of surviving as a species.

6.Resolve

LIVE AND LET LIVE. Instead, being morally obligated to save creatures from extinction, it's more like preserving your own lives as every living being on earth influence us one way or the other.

WHAT GOES AROUND, COMES AROUND. Our future generations will eventually suffer the consequences of our blunders if we continue to live inconsiderately as we do now. Extinction is difficult to observe, because the baseline changes with each generation, we might not be aware of just how much of the natural world has been lost. Past generations would regard what we see as natural today as terribly damaged, and what we see as damaged today, our children will view as natural.

Though it may seem far off, mass extinction is actually very close. Even if you don't care about protecting endangered species or have no interest in animals, this does not give you permission to do nothing. You still need to take action since there will be numerous negative effects if endangered animals go extinct. In other words, despite the fact that animals are beautiful to look at, biodiversity is significant because each species is a component of a larger system.

For example, present day there are about 20,000 bee species worldwide and around 200,000 species of flowering plants rely on bee pollination in some capacity. If you come across a lovely, fragrant plant with blue or yellow flowers, bee pollination is most likely responsible. Nearly all of these flowering plants would become extinct if bees disappeared. Grass and the majority of non-tropical trees would still exist. However, the world would be less vibrant and all the creatures and fungi that depend on those flowering plants would undoubtedly be in serious trouble.

Causes of species endangerment are many, but conservation biologists recognize that multiple forces drawn along with human activity, reinforce one another to cause a species to diminish. When people move to an area that was previously deserted, most large, sluggish, and edible animals suffer this fate.

Stories of creatures going extinct due to hunting and the subsequent deaths of their predators due to starvation because they no longer had a food source, if not from direct hunting as well, are common throughout history. The Passenger Pigeon is a well-known example of an extinct animal that was overhunted by humans, resulting in the extinction of the entire species. Currently, it is to blame for the near extinction of some well-known species, like elephants for their ivory tusks and rhinos for their horn. Because those horns are offered as a remedy for everything from hangovers to cancer at astronomical prices.

The majority of the species that originally lived in the world's former tropical forests still exist, despite having lost more than half of them. That allows time for ecological restoration to at least slow the losses. That might affect nature's existence and the services it offers in a more direct and significant way.

Ecosystems are highly localised systems built on the specific interactions of certain creatures. It may be arguable how much the total number of species on the globe matters to nature. However, it is evident that the importance of regional biodiversity is enormous.

There is a complex network of life that includes every plant, animal, and their physical surroundings. Many other species, especially humans, who depend on marine, estuarine, and riverine ecosystems for food, trade, healthcare, and recreation, may be impacted by the loss of a single species. In addition to these useful advantages, the diversity of species present in our oceans and shores inspires, beautifies, and comforts many people.

Threats to threatened and endangered species include habitat loss, disease, competition from invading species, the effects of pollution, a changing climate, and heavy or illegal harvesting pressures. Even though the primary dangers to some of the listed species are no longer present, there aren't enough of the species' individuals left to significantly reduce the probability of extinction to the point where the species is no longer in danger of going extinct. Recovery is the process of restoring endangered and threatened species to the point where they no longer require the safeguards.

Numerous animals must cross a landscape filled with human threats since they reside in developed regions. Roads are one of the major barriers to wildlife surviving in urban environments. For every animal seeking to cross from one side of a habitat to the other, roads pose a constant risk. So, one needs to slow down and watch out for wildlife when they are out and about.

The protection of endangered species is becoming more and more difficult due to climate change. In addition to having a direct impact on our plants and animals through variations in temperature and precipitation, for example climate change has the potential to exacerbate the effects of existing threats to endangered species, such as invasive species, wildfires, and illnesses.

An effective and internationally recognized strategy for conserving species and ecosystems is to designate protected areas. A protected area as an area of land or sea especially dedicated to the protection of biological diversity and of natural and associated cultural resources, managed through legal or other effective means. There are many different types of protected places around the world, each with their own management goals and level of protection, such as national parks, state/provincial parks, wildlife refuges, and nature reserves.

De-extinction, often known as resurrection biology, is the technique of bringing back extinct or extinctive organisms. Advances in selective breeding, genetics, and reproductive cloning technology have raised the potential of reviving extinct species, which was formerly thought to be a fantastical idea. A clone was created using the preserved tissues, however it passed away shortly after birth due to a serious lung abnormality. The attempts near success generated discussion over whether or not species should be saved from extinction and, if so, how it should be done and how the species should be managed.

Early in the 20th century, the prospect of reviving extinct species was investigated using a technique called reverse breeding or breeding back. The principles of selective breeding, which people have used for ages to create animals with desirable features, are the foundation of back breeding, which aims to create a breed that exhibits the traits of a wild progenitor.

German zoologists Lutz and Heinz Heck attempted to back breed for an animal that resembled the aurochs, an extinct species of European wild ox related to current cattle, in the early 20th century by crossing several breeds of cattle. Based on historical accounts and bone specimens that provide morphological details about the aurochs but no knowledge of the animals' genetic relatedness, the Heck brothers interbred modern cattle. As a result, the Heck cattle that were produced but were not very similar to aurochs.

The ability to separate and analyse DNA from the bones, hair, and other tissues of dead animals was made possible by the development of instruments in the second half of the 20th century. Researchers were able to select cattle that are near genetic cousins of the aurochs and mix their sperm and eggs to create an animal that is morphologically and genetically identical to the aurochs thanks to advancements in reproductive technologies like in vitro fertilisation.

Cloning refers to the technique known as somatic cell nuclear transfer to create an exact genetic copy of a living organism. In the cloning process, the host egg cell reprograms the adult somatic cell's nucleus once it has been injected into a detached egg cell. The somatic cell is transformed into an undifferentiated pluripotent stem cell by this reprogramming, allowing it to develop in a manner similar to how an embryo would after being fertilised by a sperm cell and an egg cell. The nuclear genome sequence of the organism created through cloning will be identical to that of the somatic cell donor.

Cloning is a desirable method for preventing extinction since, unlike back-breeding, the new organism will be identical to the extinct donor of the somatic cell, at least in terms of the nuclear genome. However, most extinct species lack the intact live cells needed for cloning, which are not present in them. When an organism dies, the DNA contained in its tissues starts to degrade almost instantly so in many cases cloning is not possible.

When used to prevent extinction, sophisticated technologies like cloning, stem cell research, genome editing, and genome reconstruction have substantial ethical implications. The potential for those technologies and back breeding to change the trajectory of natural history, though, is perhaps the biggest worry. De-extinction offers mankind the chance to make up for past wrongs done to other species and increase species variety.

But many extinct species were wiped out due to habitat loss, while others lived in ecosystems that have undergone significant changes since they were alive. Additionally, revived species would be regarded as endangered in the near future and would consequently need conservation, for which resources are sometimes limited or non-existent.

Other concerns relate to the unknowns surrounding the fate of revived animals, such as the health of cloned individuals, the animals' ability to adapt to the environment, and the animals' ability to have viable offspring. It is also unclear how to classify species that have been brought back to life through back-breeding, cloning, or genetic reconstruction, all of which may have diverged from the genetic makeup of the extinct species. Some have questioned the motives of researchers and businesses behind some de-extinction efforts due to the possibility of using them to advance financial and commercial objectives.

The researchers of a study fear that the next mass extinction is also in process due to the widespread rejection of science that is occurring in modern day society. Some people even argue that the extinctions are just a new and natural evolutionary trajectory, although one that is created by only one species on earth, humans.

Here are some measures you can take to safeguard threatened species and stop their extinction, including consumption of less meat. One of the greatest contributors to deforestation is the production of soybeans, and the majority of soybean meal is utilised as animal feed. Because organic farmers only use natural or non-synthetic pesticides on their crops, buy organic food. Other creatures may be hazardous when exposed to synthetic pesticides.

For ethical eating, pick sustainable seafood, such as some species of cheap fish. Compost food waste because urban farming and gardening, which offer habitat for pollinators, utilise compost. Avoid purchasing items such as tortoise shell, ivory, coral, some animal skins, and traditional medicines that come from endangered or threatened species.

Two of the biggest causes of our ever-growing list of endangered species are deforestation and climate change, and the vast majority of this is caused by global warming and us infringing on animal habitats. We can all help even in small ways by putting our planet first. You can find endangered creatures almost everywhere, so familiarise yourself with the best practises for safeguarding them and perhaps study up on any national wildlife refuges that you can help.

Because the ivory trade is lucrative, organisations like Coalition Wildlife Trafficking internet do critical and vital work to prevent the internet sale of endangered animals and to keep native wildlife in its natural habitat. If you're buying presents for family members or friends back home, be sure they're made of environmentally friendly materials that won't threaten or worse, exterminate, endangered species.

There are a huge number of organizations that specialize in Endangered species conservation such as the Wild Animal Health Fund. Their sole purpose is to ensure the protection of any species whether it be an animal or plant that is endangered.

They put forth a lot of effort in investigating the reasons why native landscapes are deteriorating and assisting threatened species to return to their natural environment. These kinds of institutions enable nature to resist its biggest threat, humans. These problems would not have arisen in the first place if we treated all animals with the love and respect they merit.

Finally, on earth every living being is either directly or indirectly dependent on the rest of living beings, so even if we think that extinction of one or two species will not make much difference then we are wrong. Everything has its own purpose to fulfil and role they play in the cycle of time, so one missing link in that process may lead to greater effects which may affect us greatly if coming times.

As we can't reverse what has happened, we can only try to protect which are currently endangered and strive along with technology to bring back the species which went extinct from endangered, which can at least help us atone for our actions towards the other living beings on earth.

Bibilography

https://naturalhistory.si.edu/education/teaching-resources/paleontology/extinction-over-time

https://www.greenpeace.org.uk/news/18-animals-that-went-extinct-in-the-last-century/

https://www.rd.com/list/animals-extinct-last-100-years/

https://www.popularmechanics.com/science/animals/g201/recently-extinct-animals-list/

https://www.onekindplanet.org/top-10/top-10-worlds-extinct-animals/

https://www.marineinsight.com/environment/10-endangered-ocean-species-and-marine-animals/

https://www.popularmechanics.com/science/animals/g183/endangered-sea-creatures-pictures-03112/

https://www.worldwildlife.org/species/directory?direction=desc&sort=extinction_status

https://www.conserve-energy-future.com/most-endangered-species-on-earth.

May I Request a Review?

Could you please leave a review of this book? I hope you have enjoyed this interesting topic. Reviews may not matter to big brand authors, but they are of tremendous help to authors like me, who are rising and do not have much of a following yet.

This will help me to increase my readership by encouraging people to take a chance on my books. When you read this book, you might like to place a review. It will take less than two minutes to write what you feel about the content. Thank you for reading and supporting my work. I'd love to see your review on the publisher page.

9 798397 083713